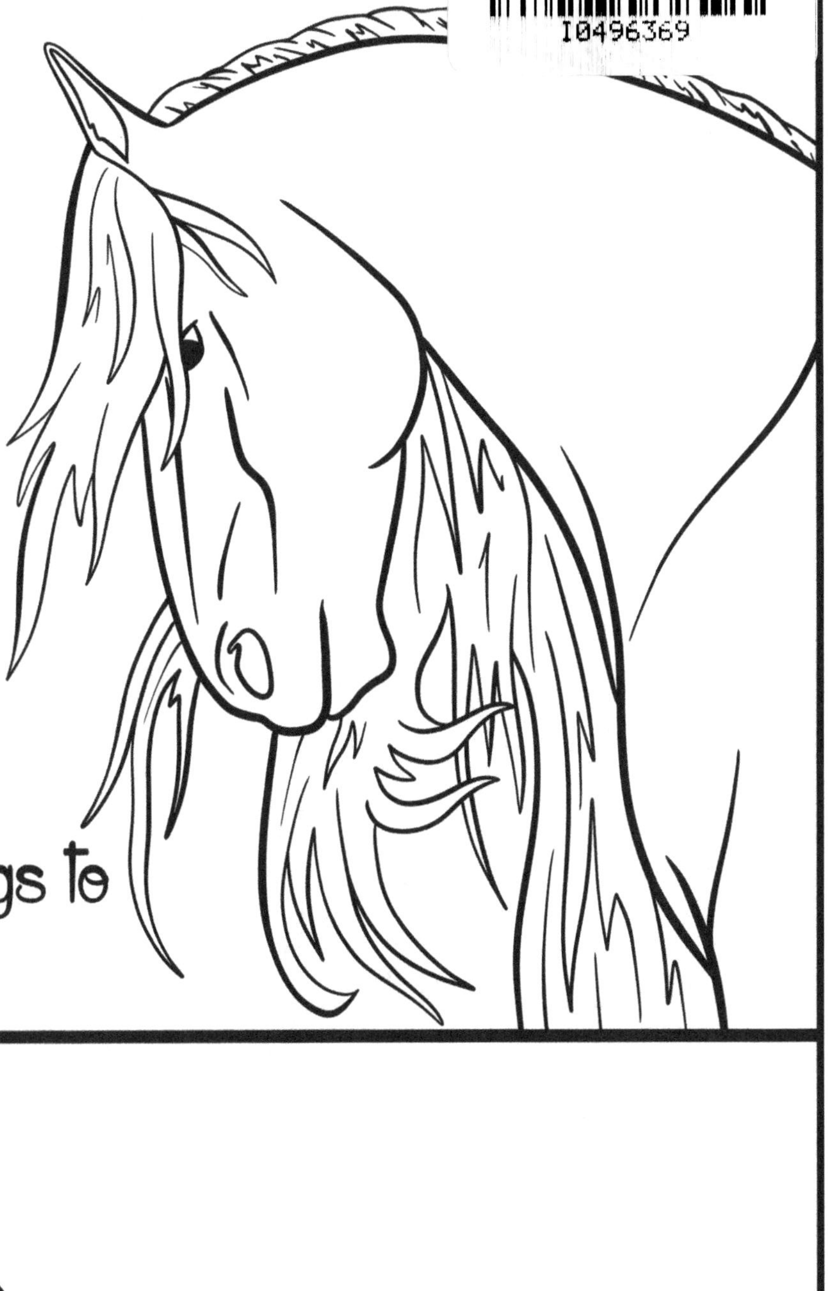

This Book Belongs to

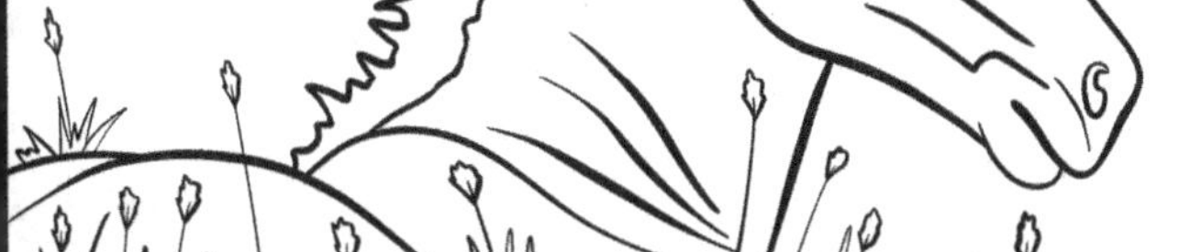

Copyright 2020 Matt Claridge
Author and Illustrator

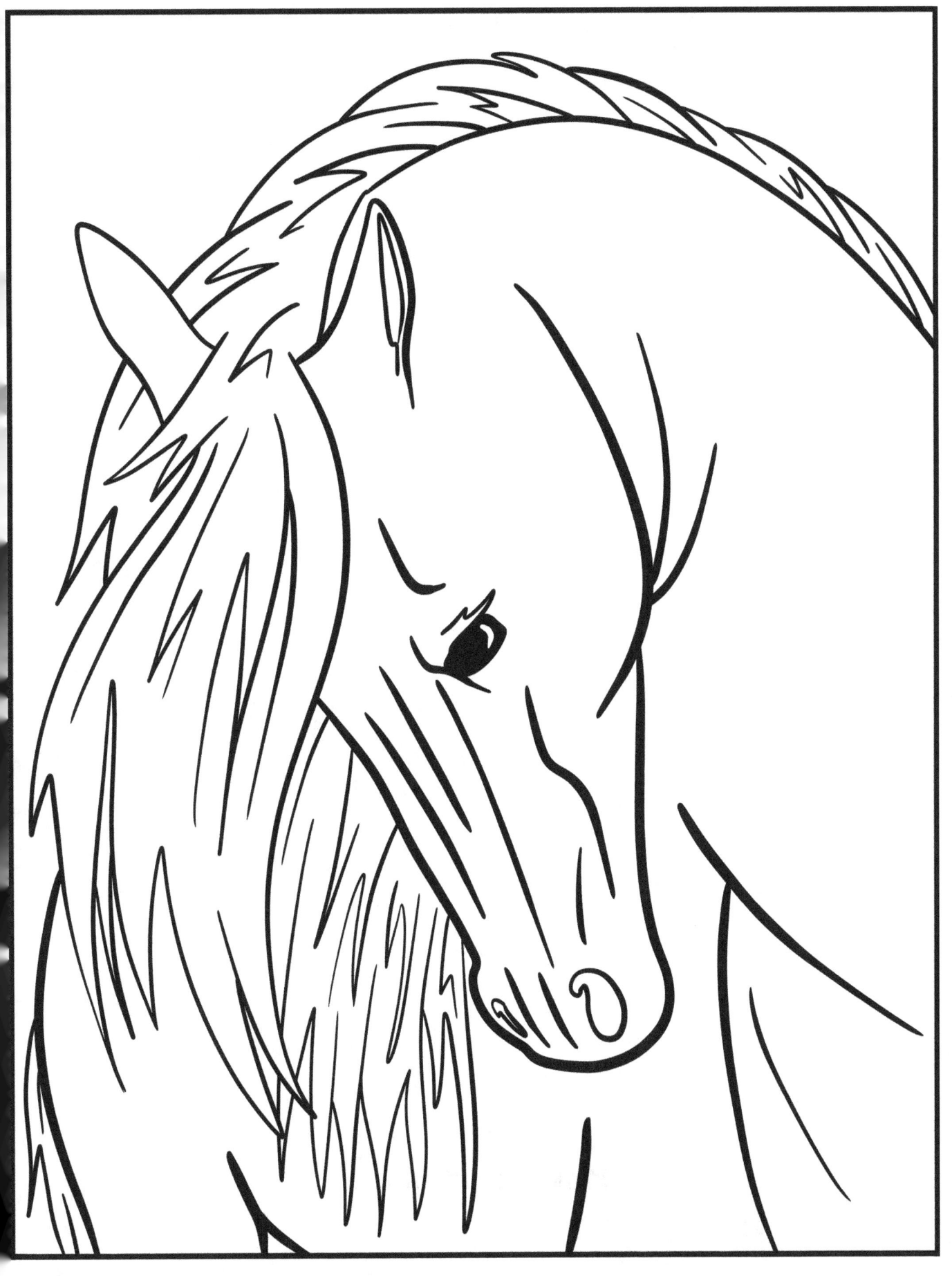

Horse and Mane

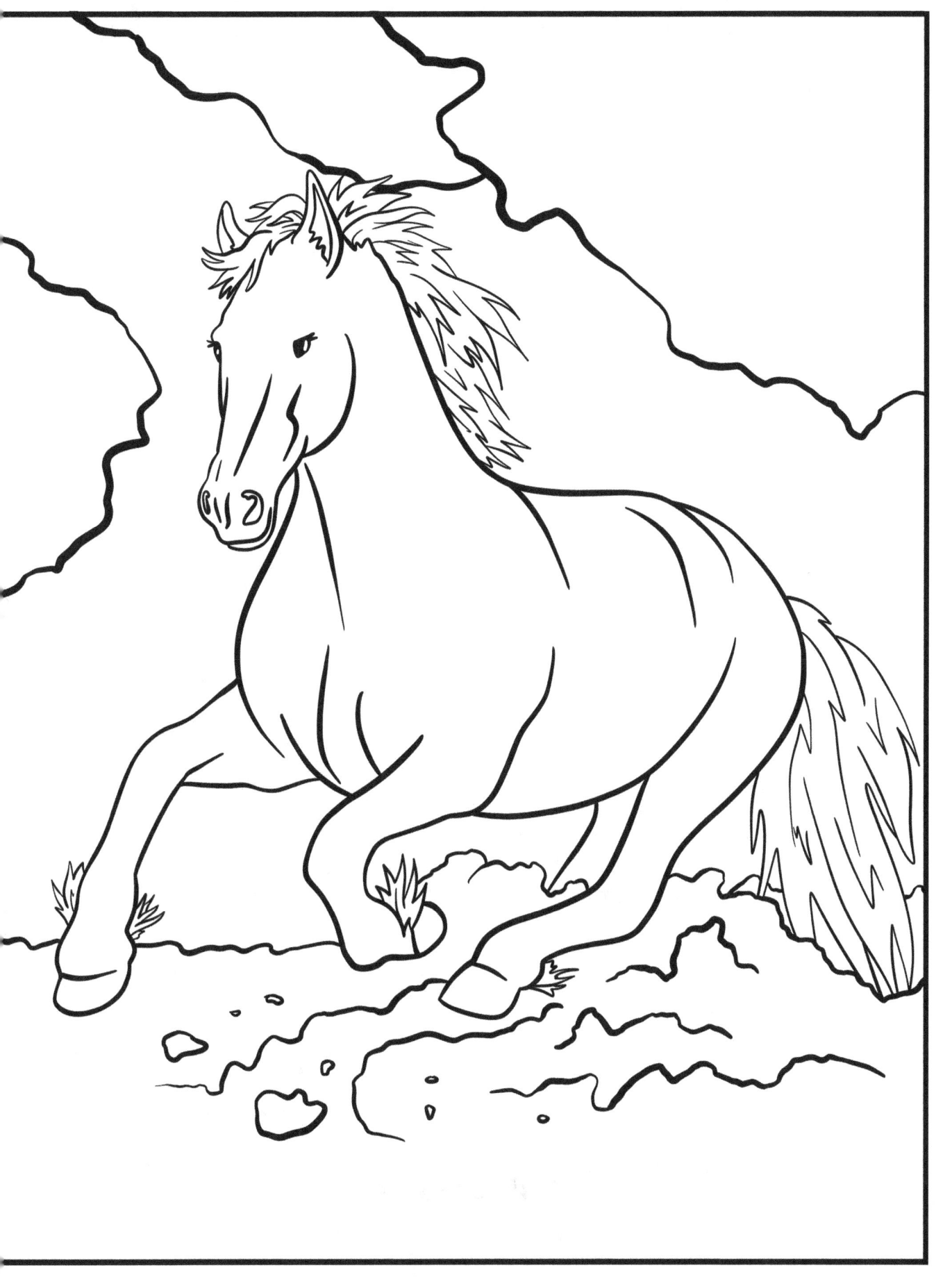

Shire Horse

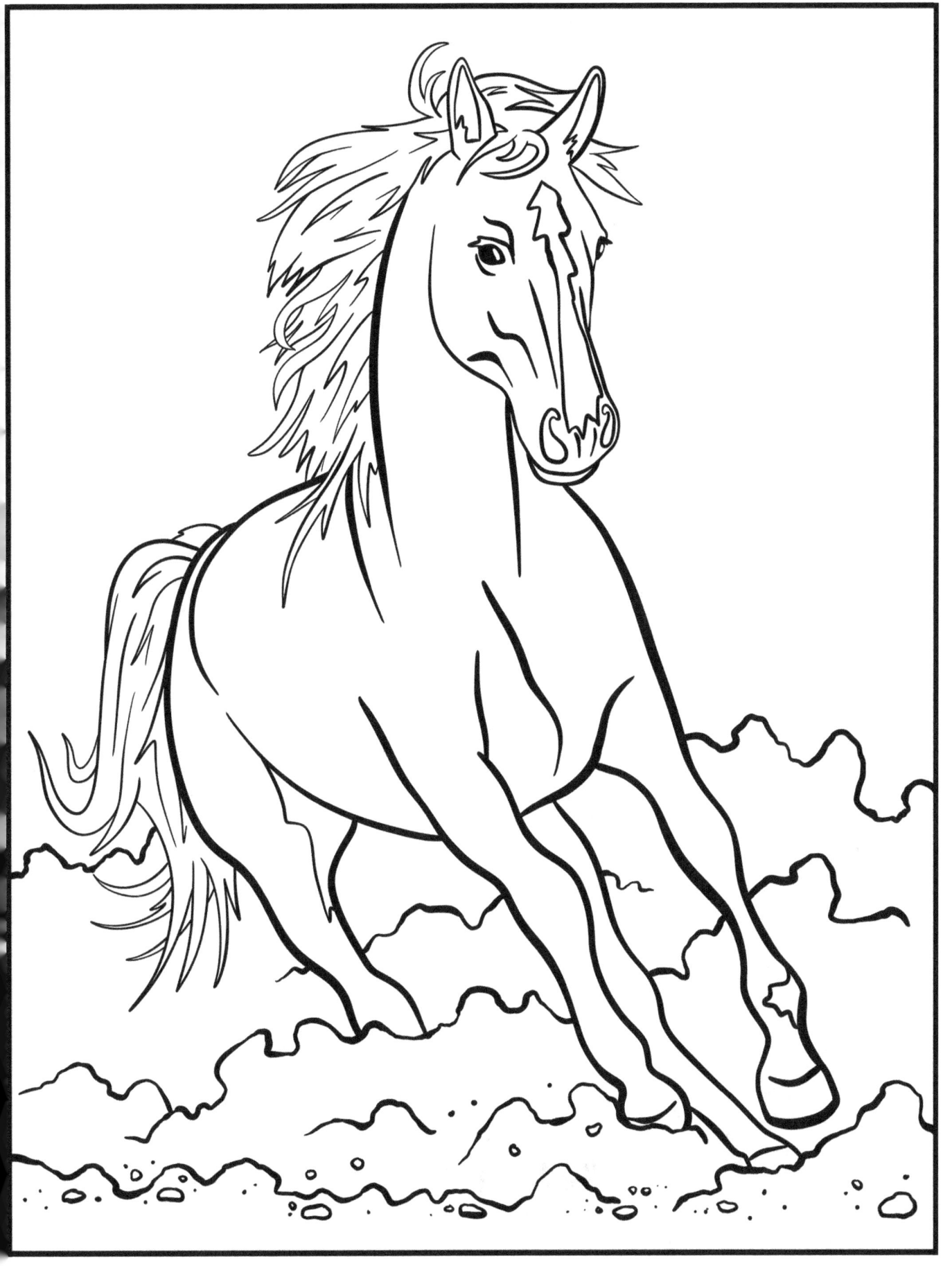

Kicking Up Dirt

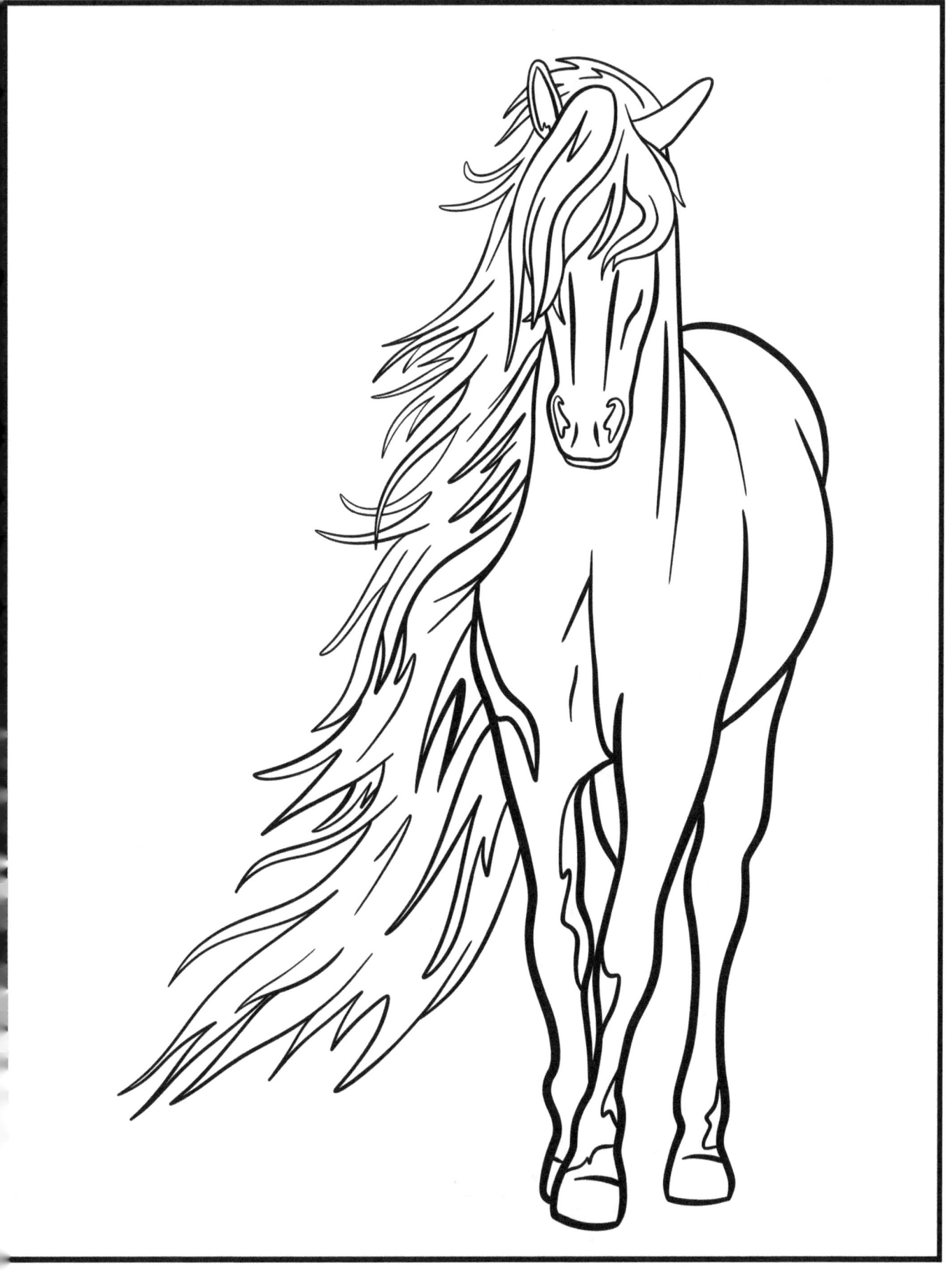

Friesian

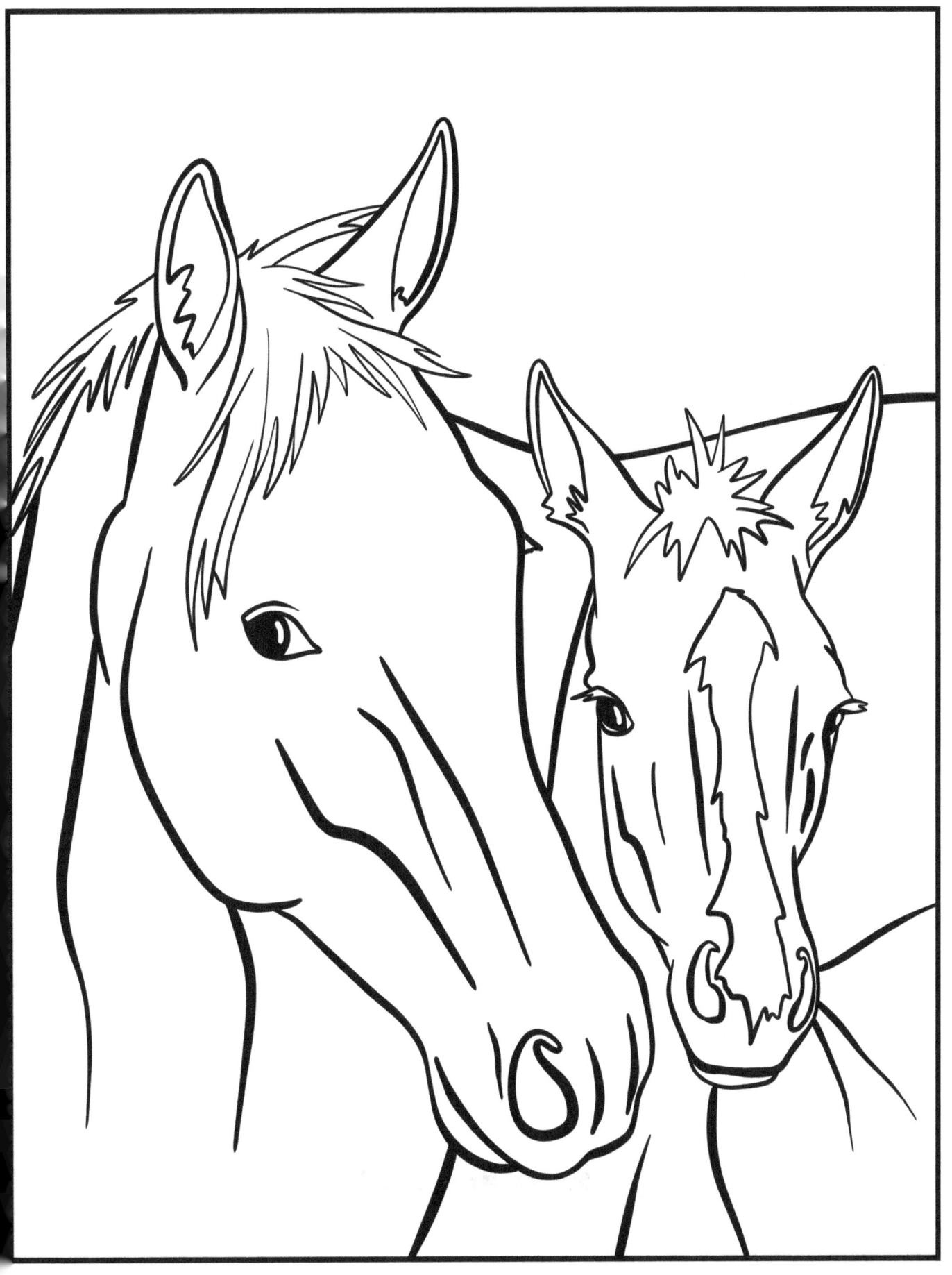

Mare and Foal

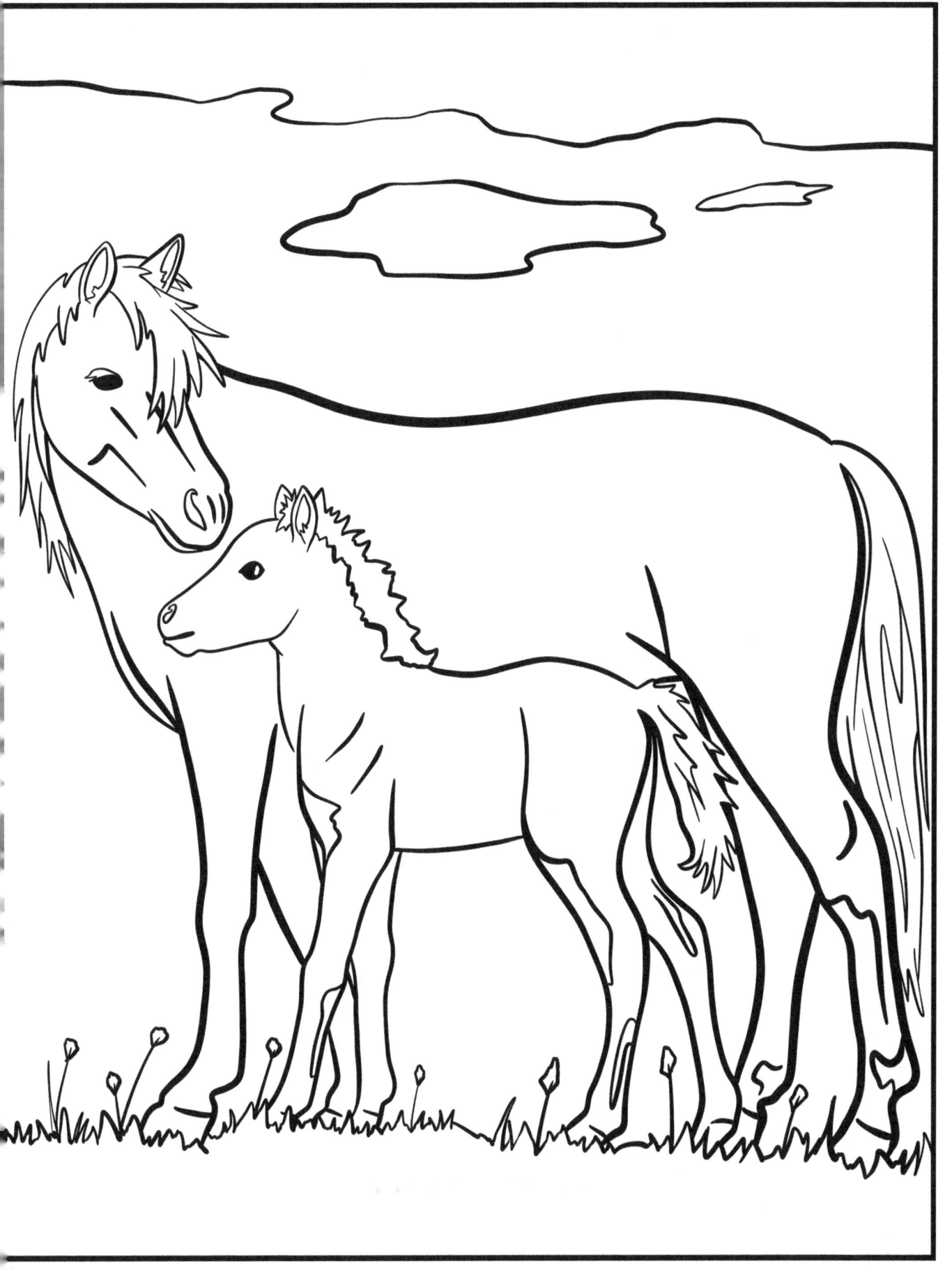

Mare and Foal

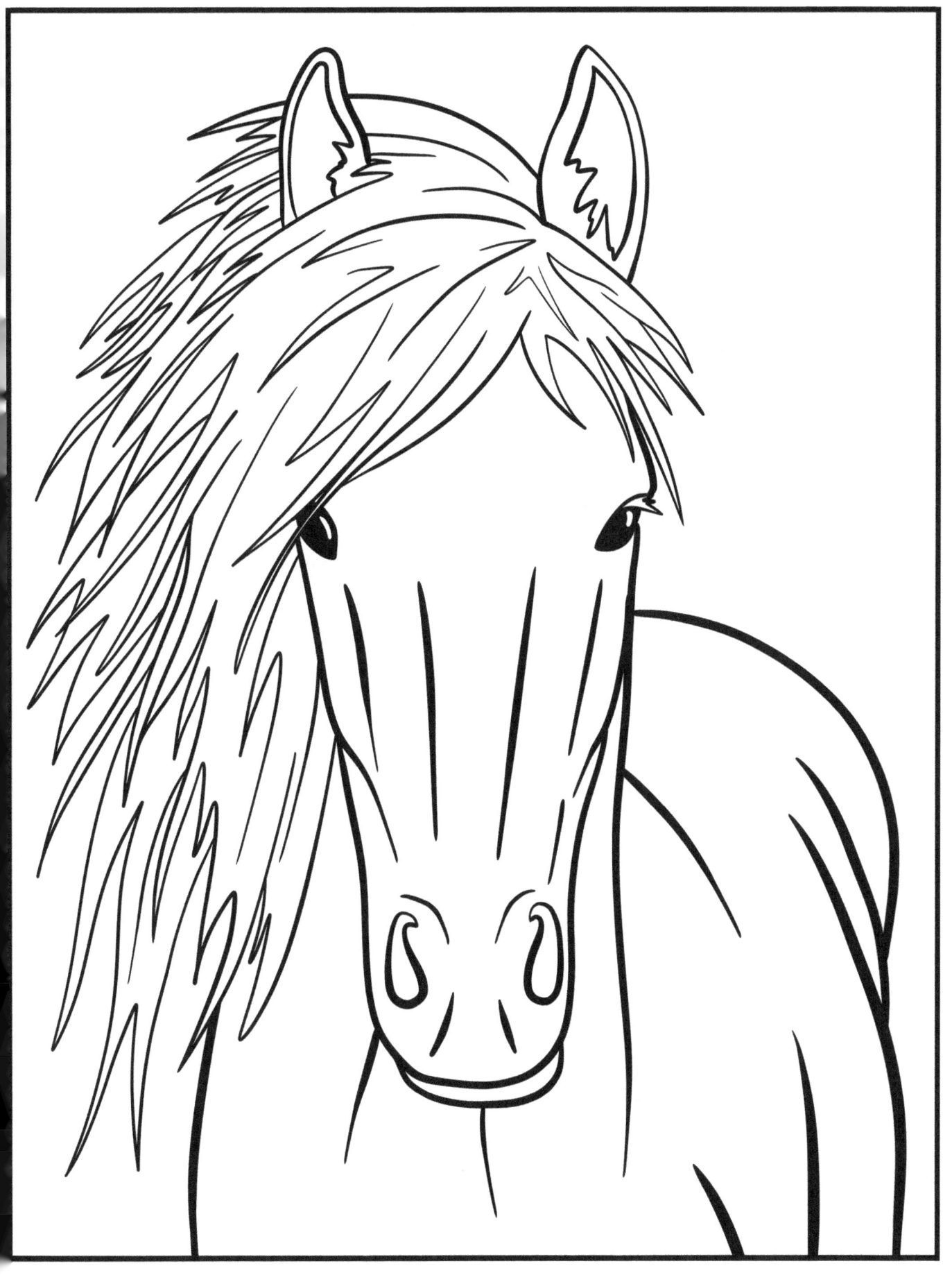

Wild Pony

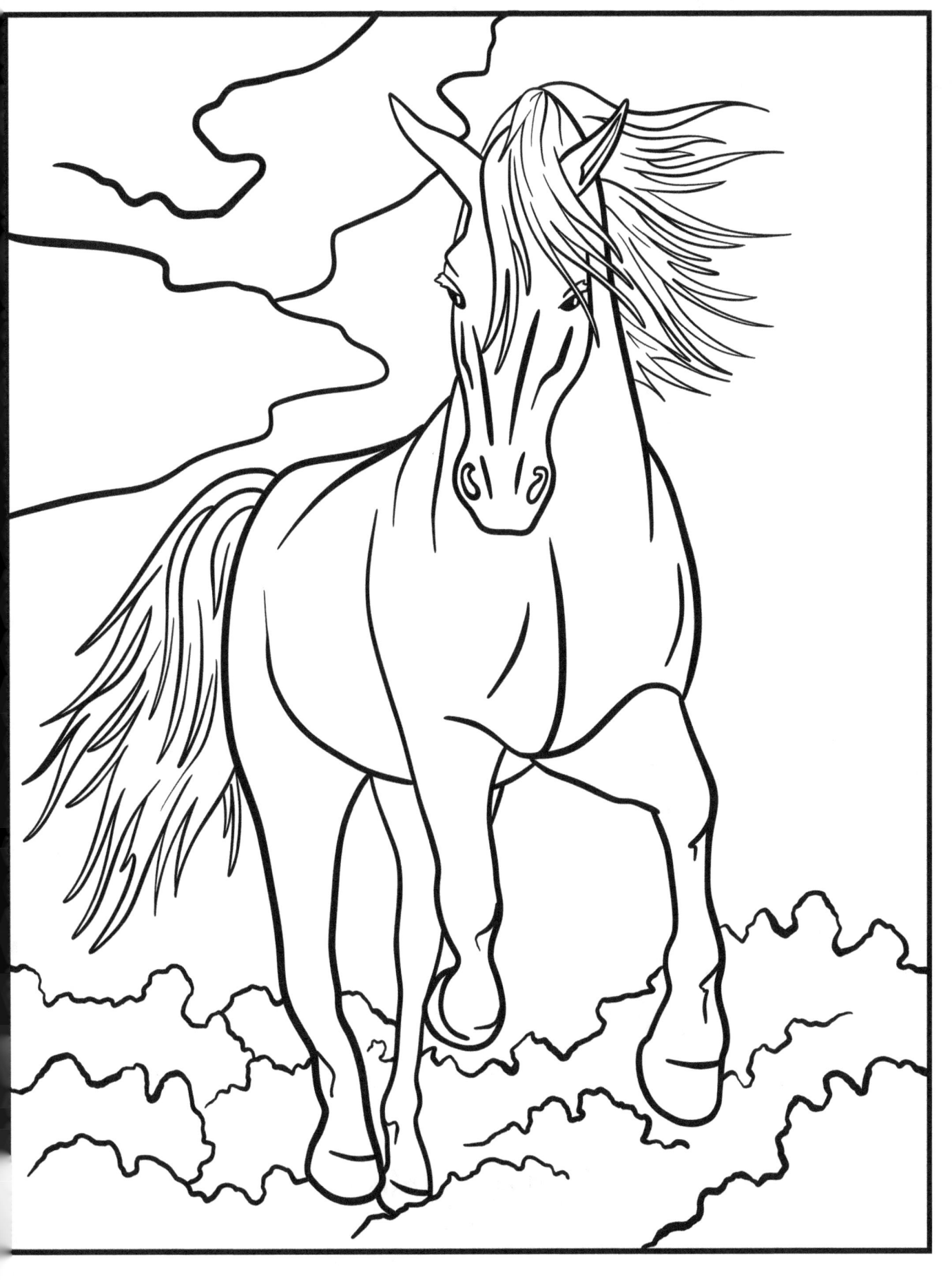

Running Stalion

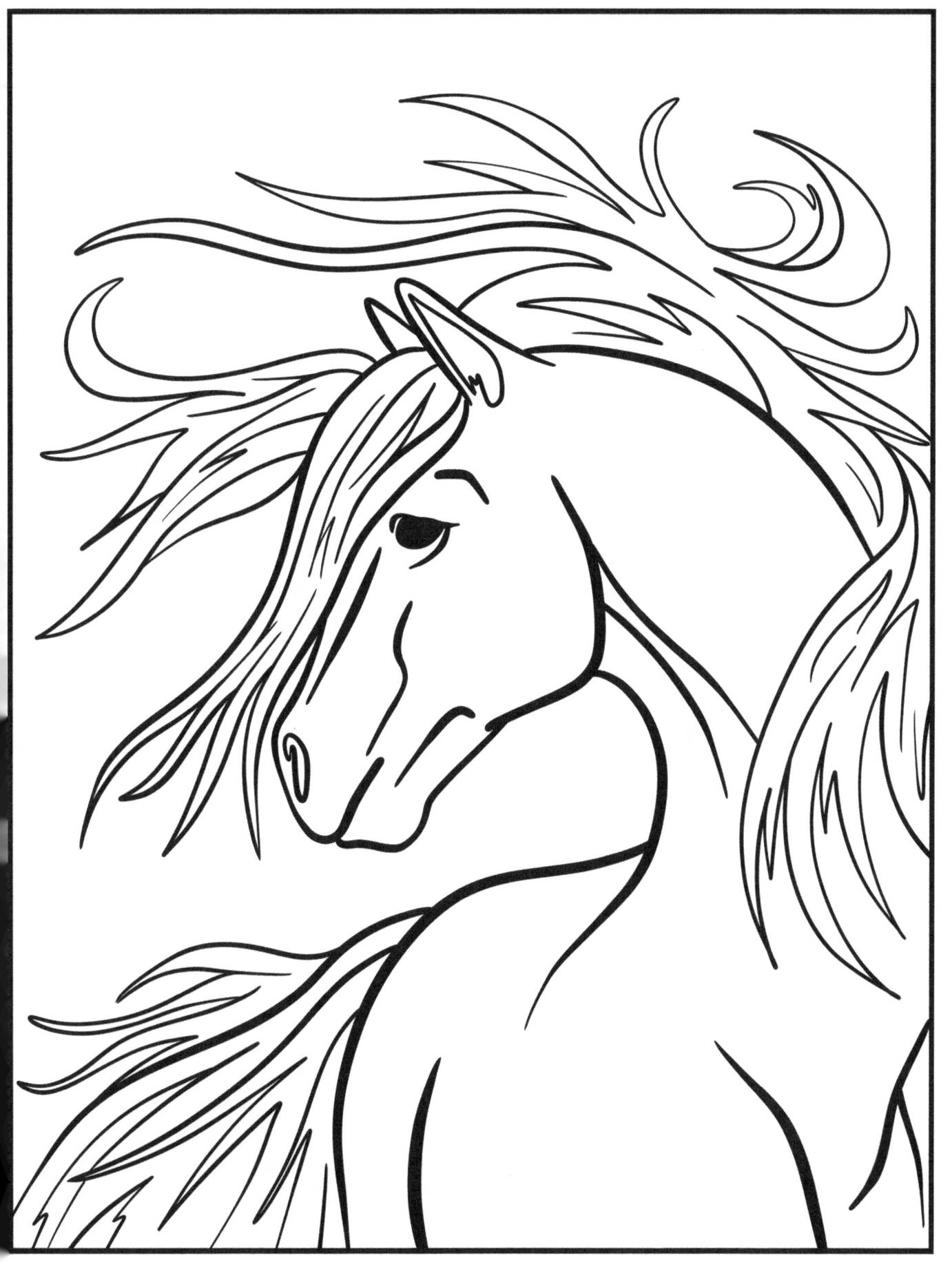

Paint

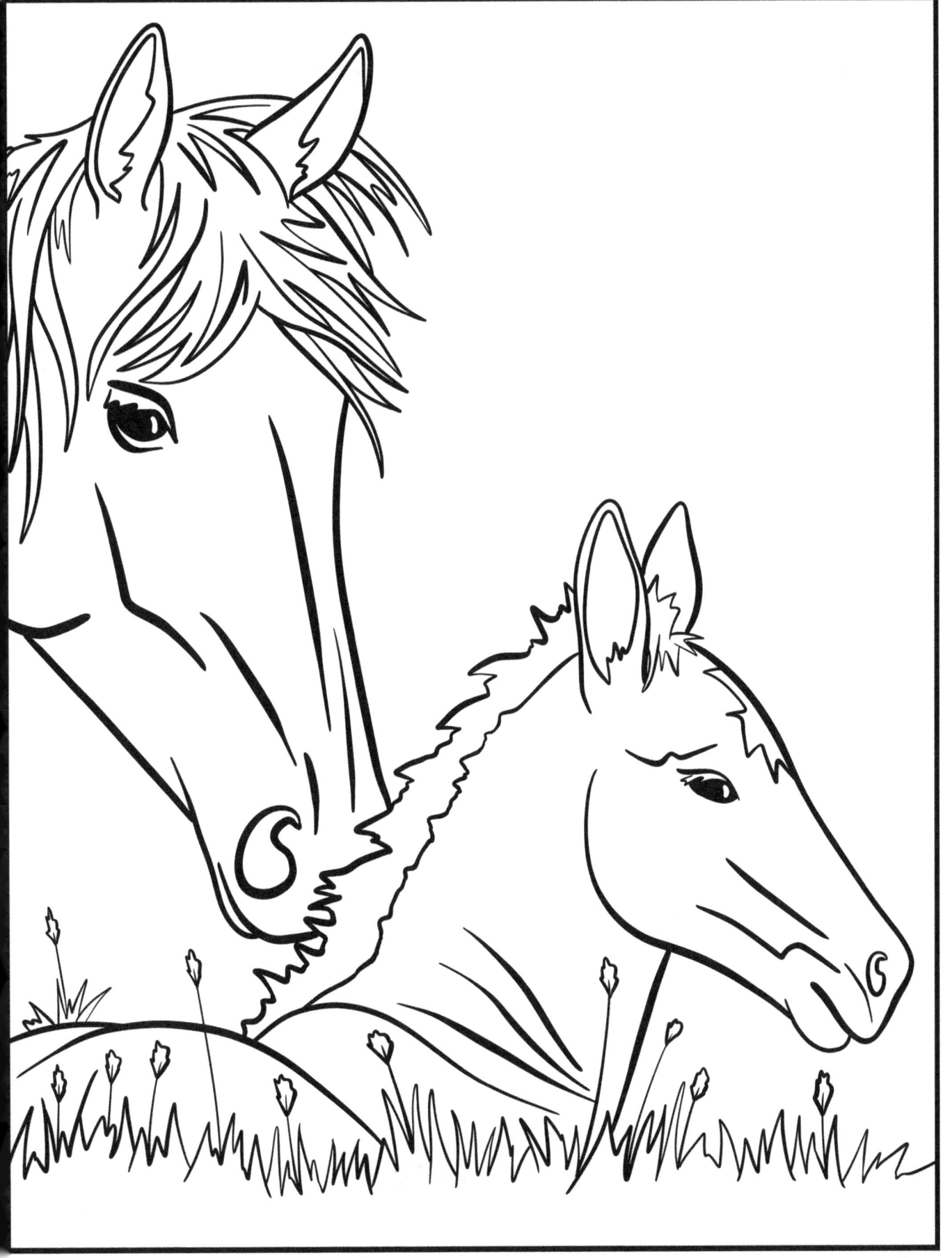

Mare and Foal

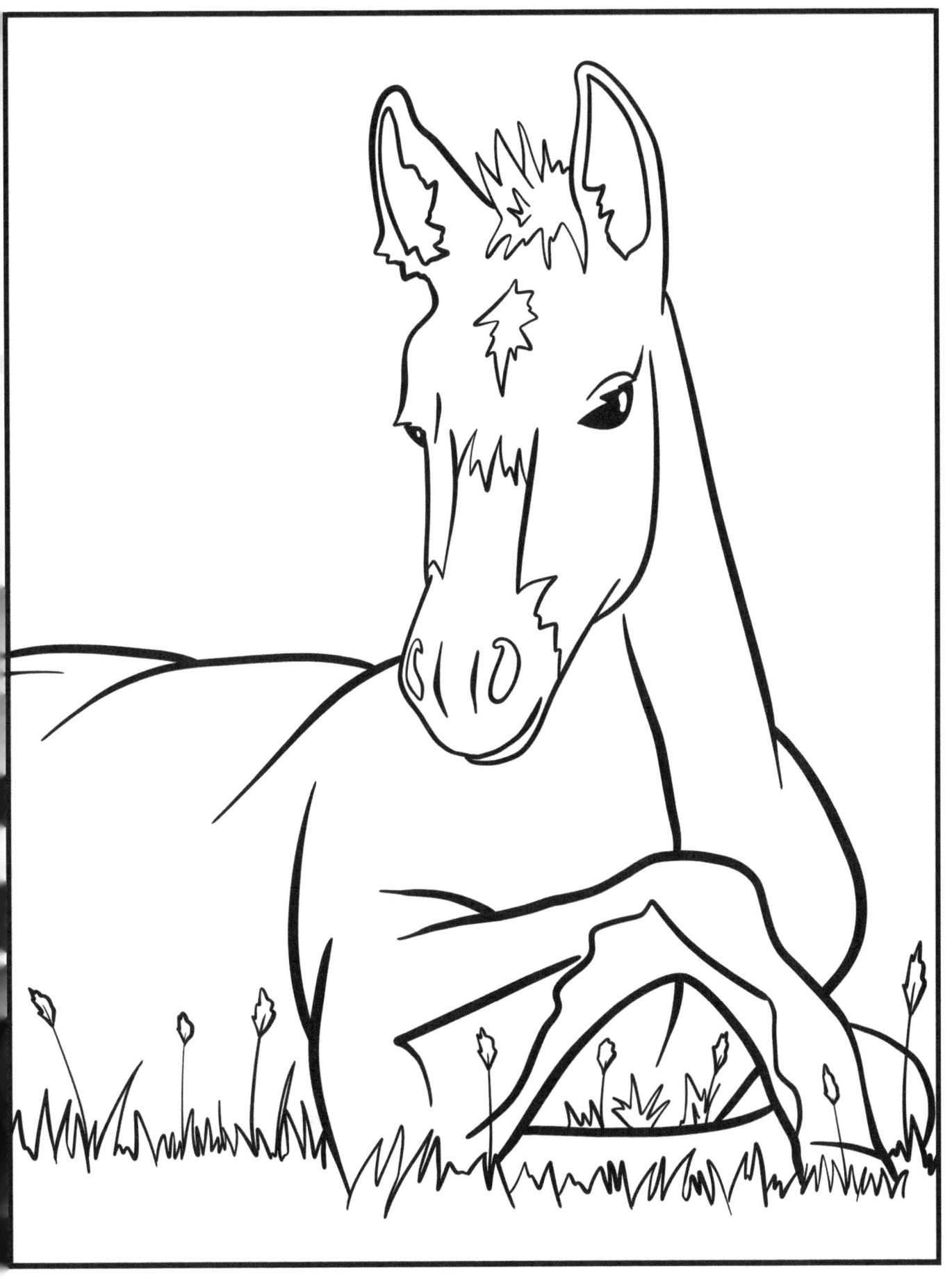

Foal

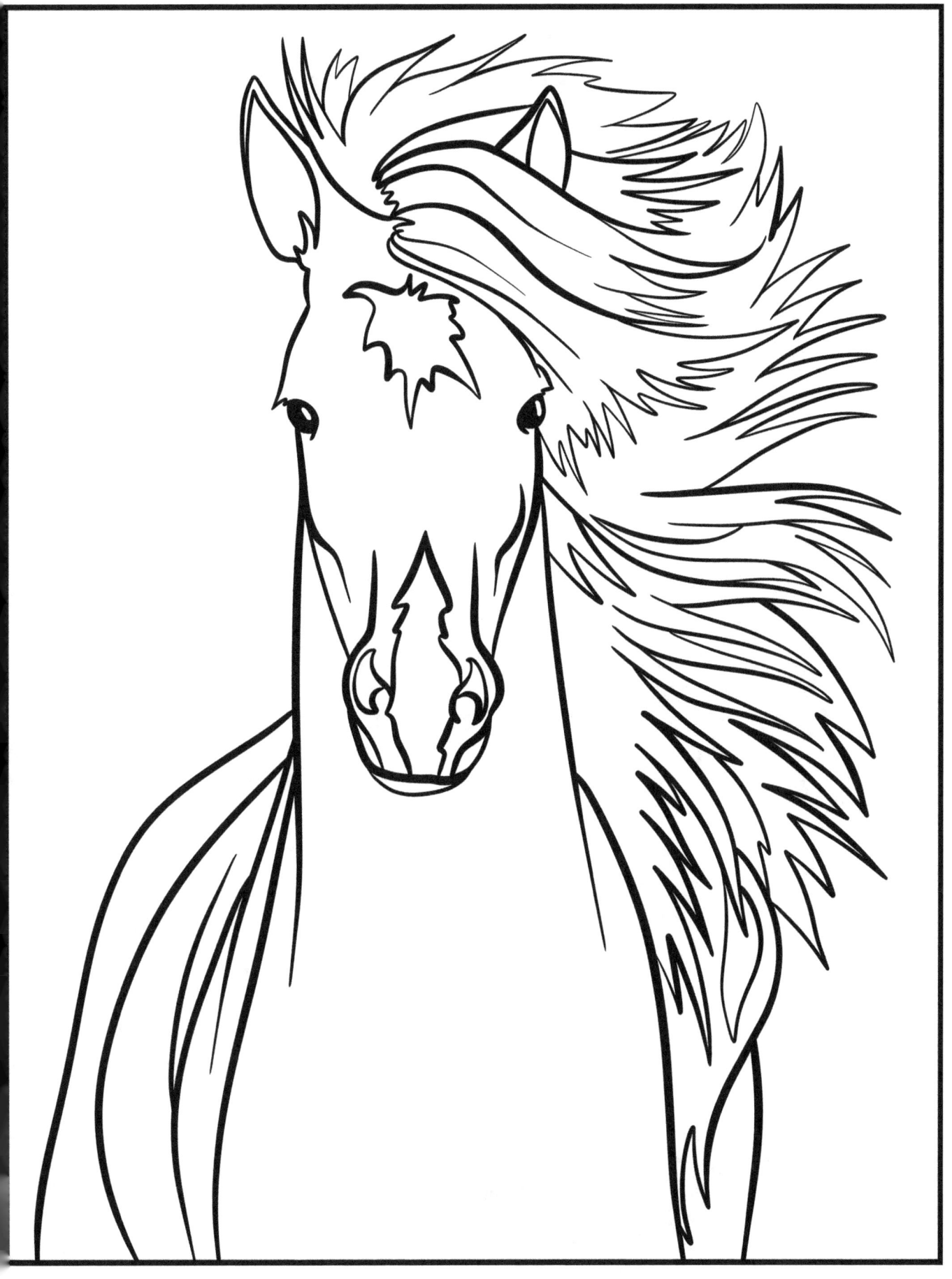

In the Wind

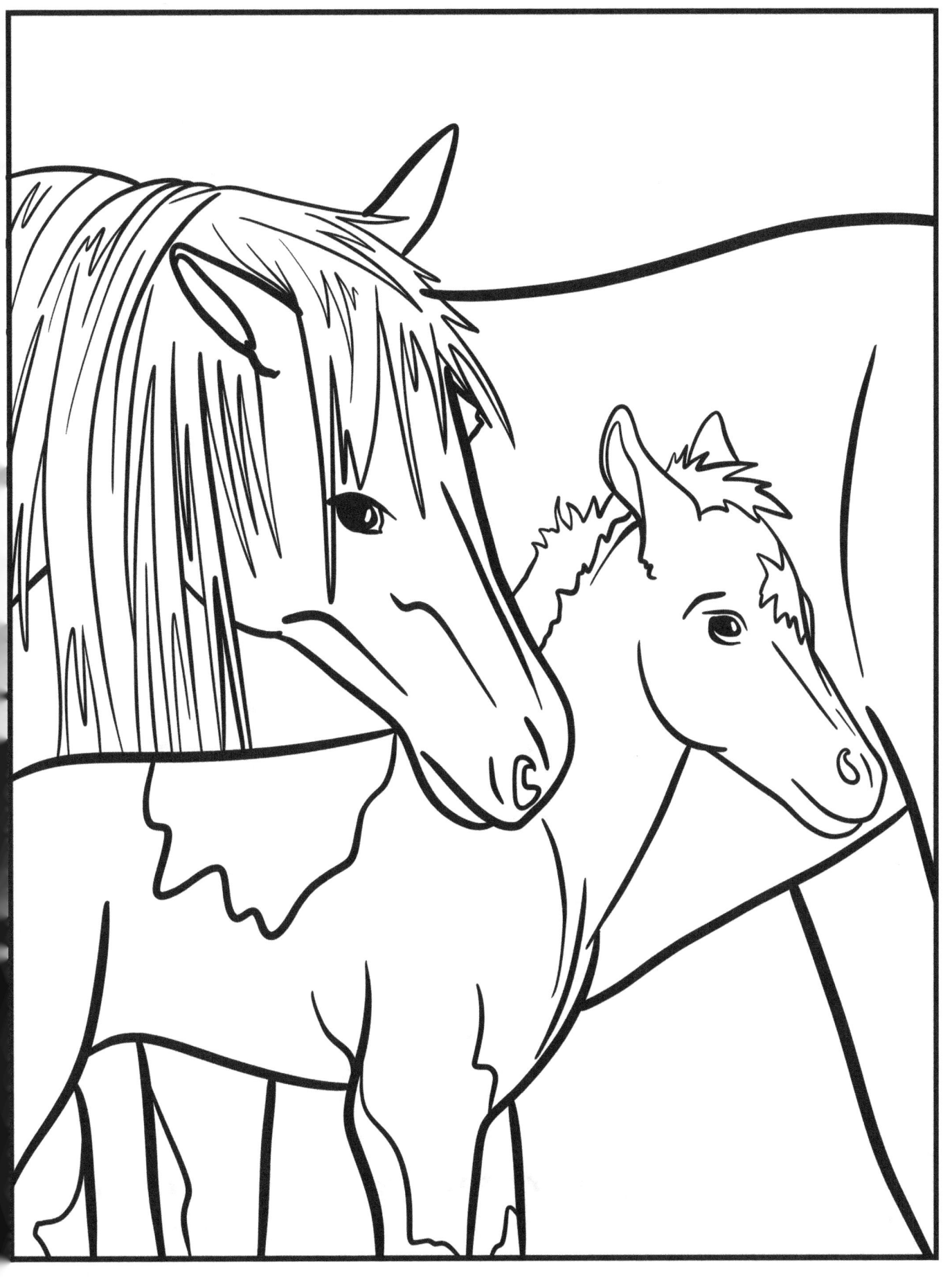

Mare and Foal

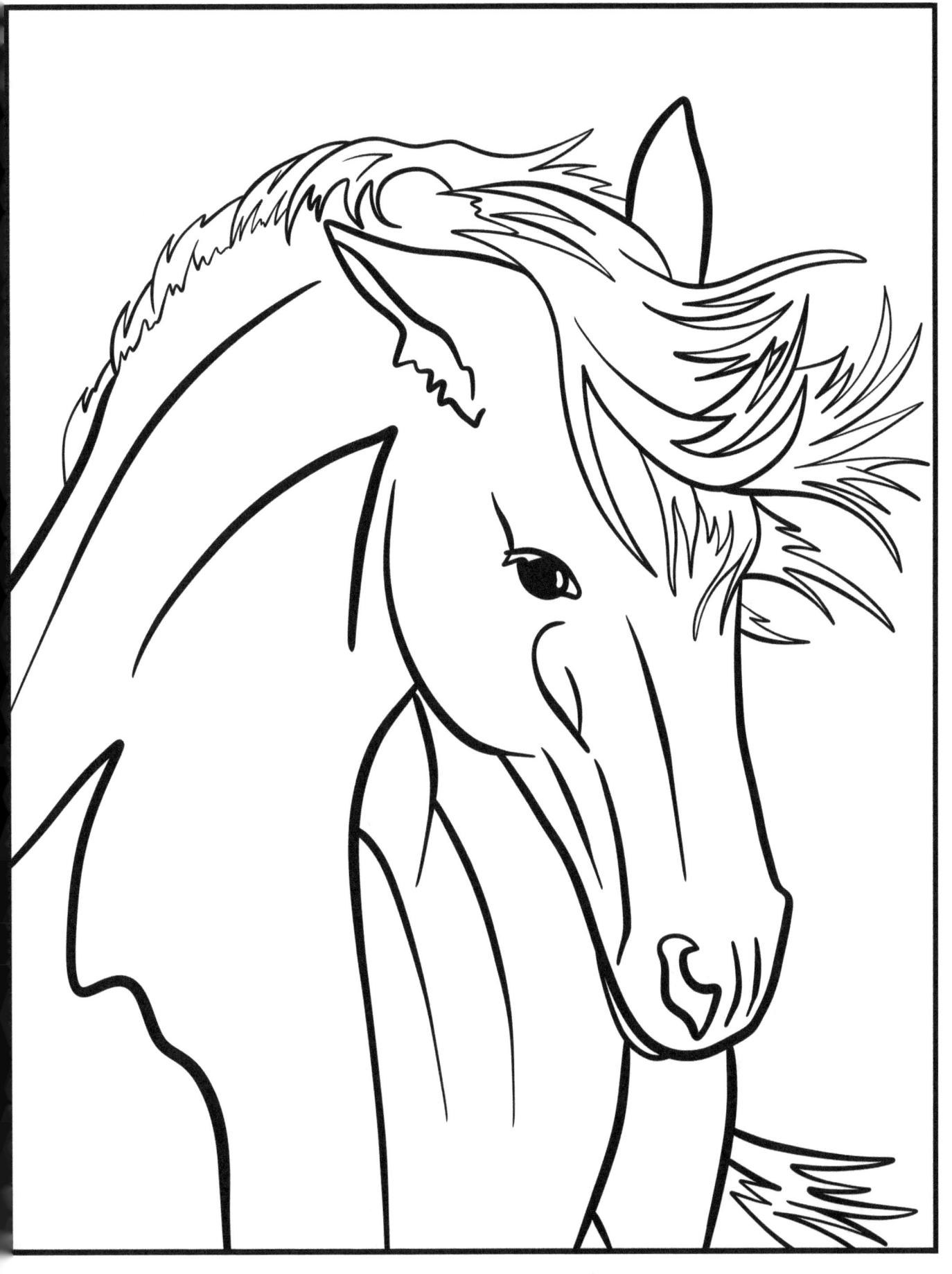

Shy

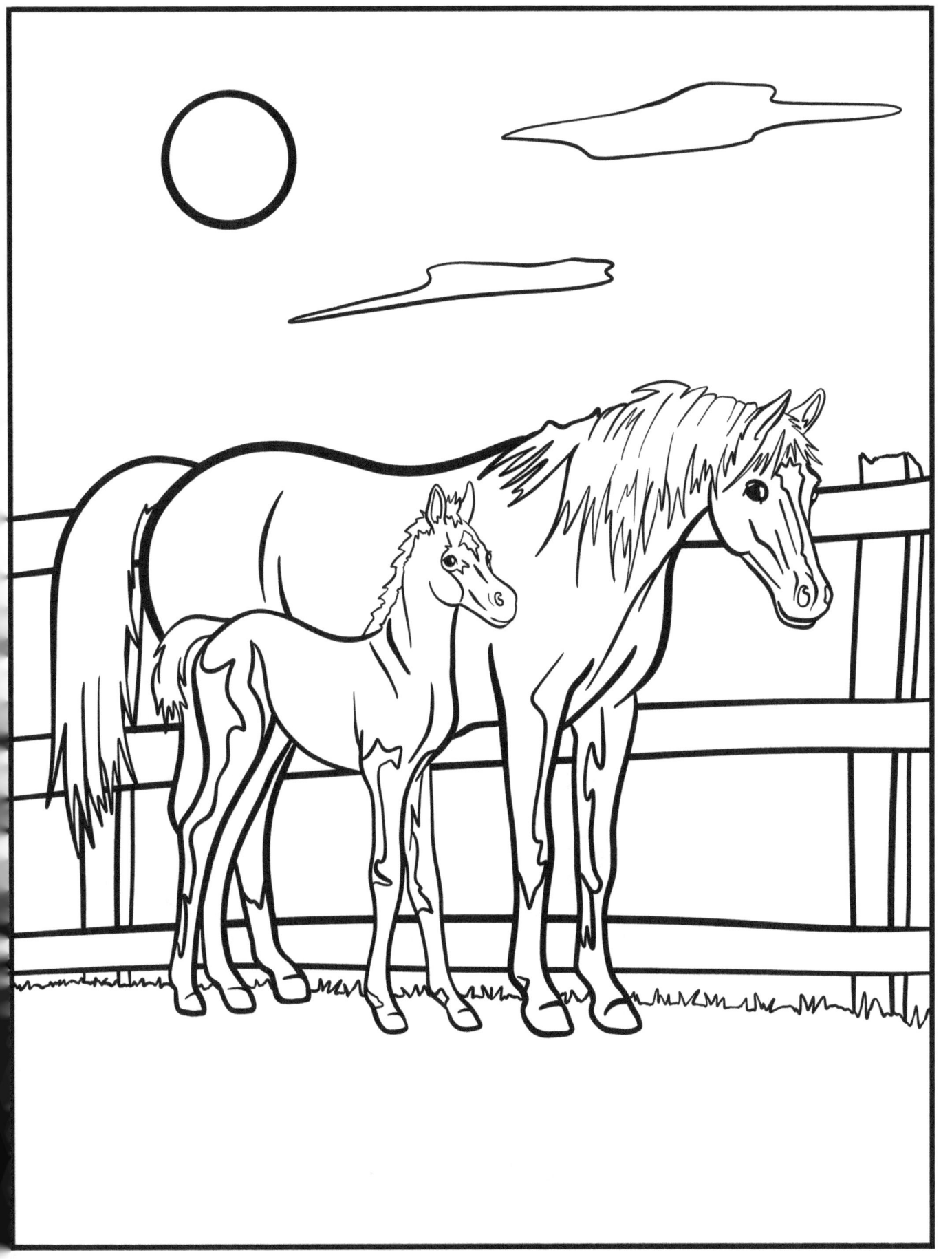

Mare and Foal

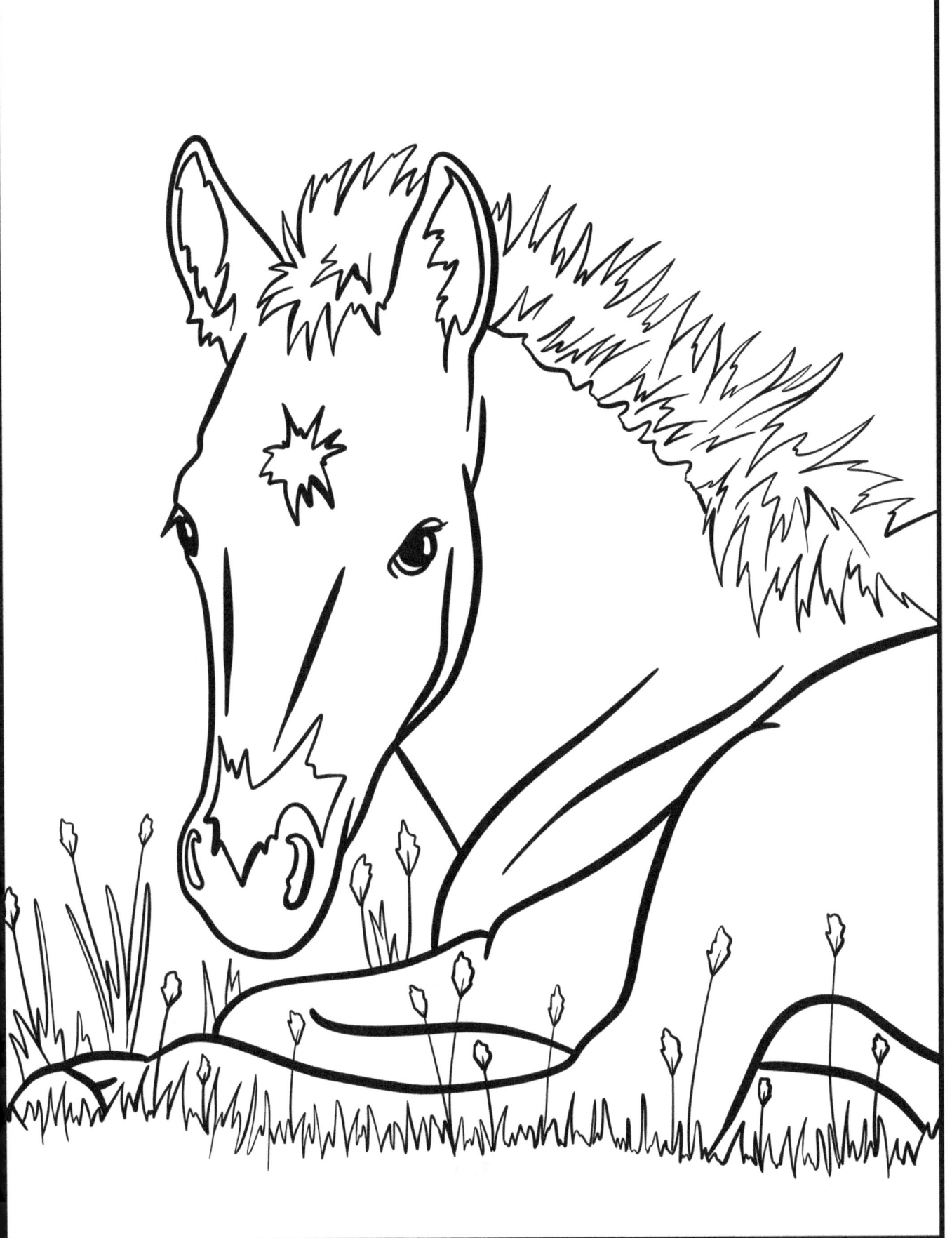

Foal

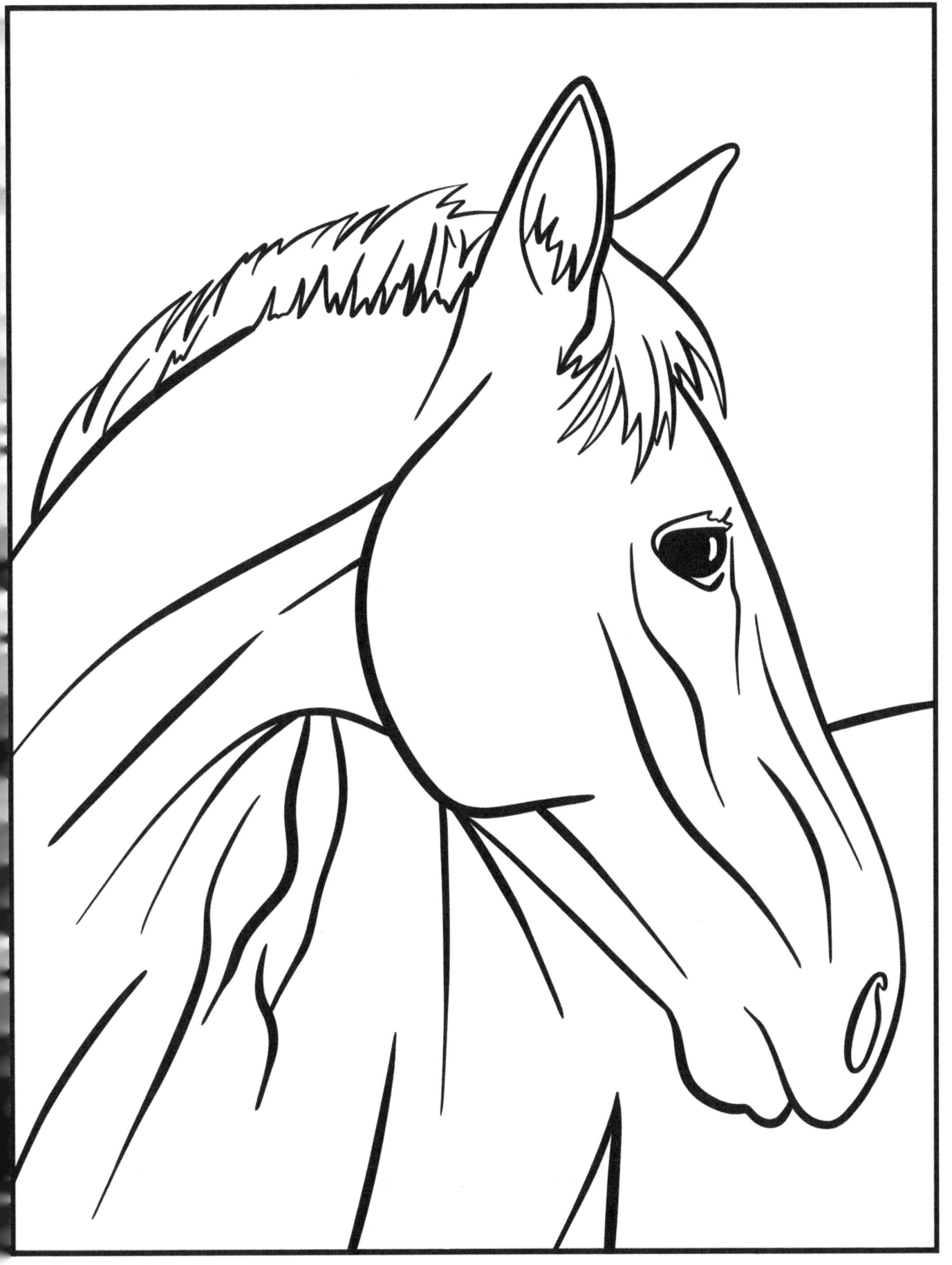

Looking Back

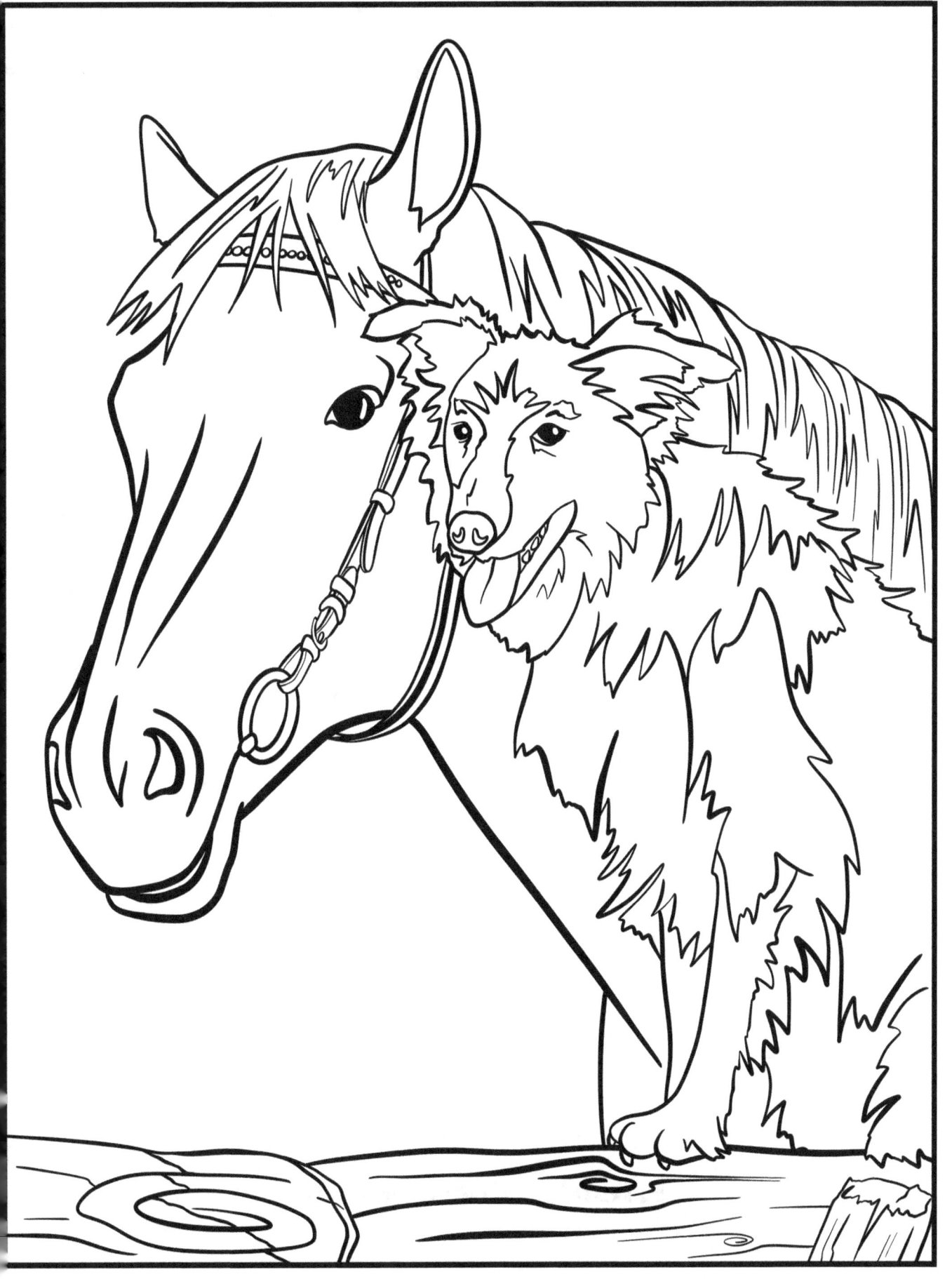

Friends - Horse and Dog

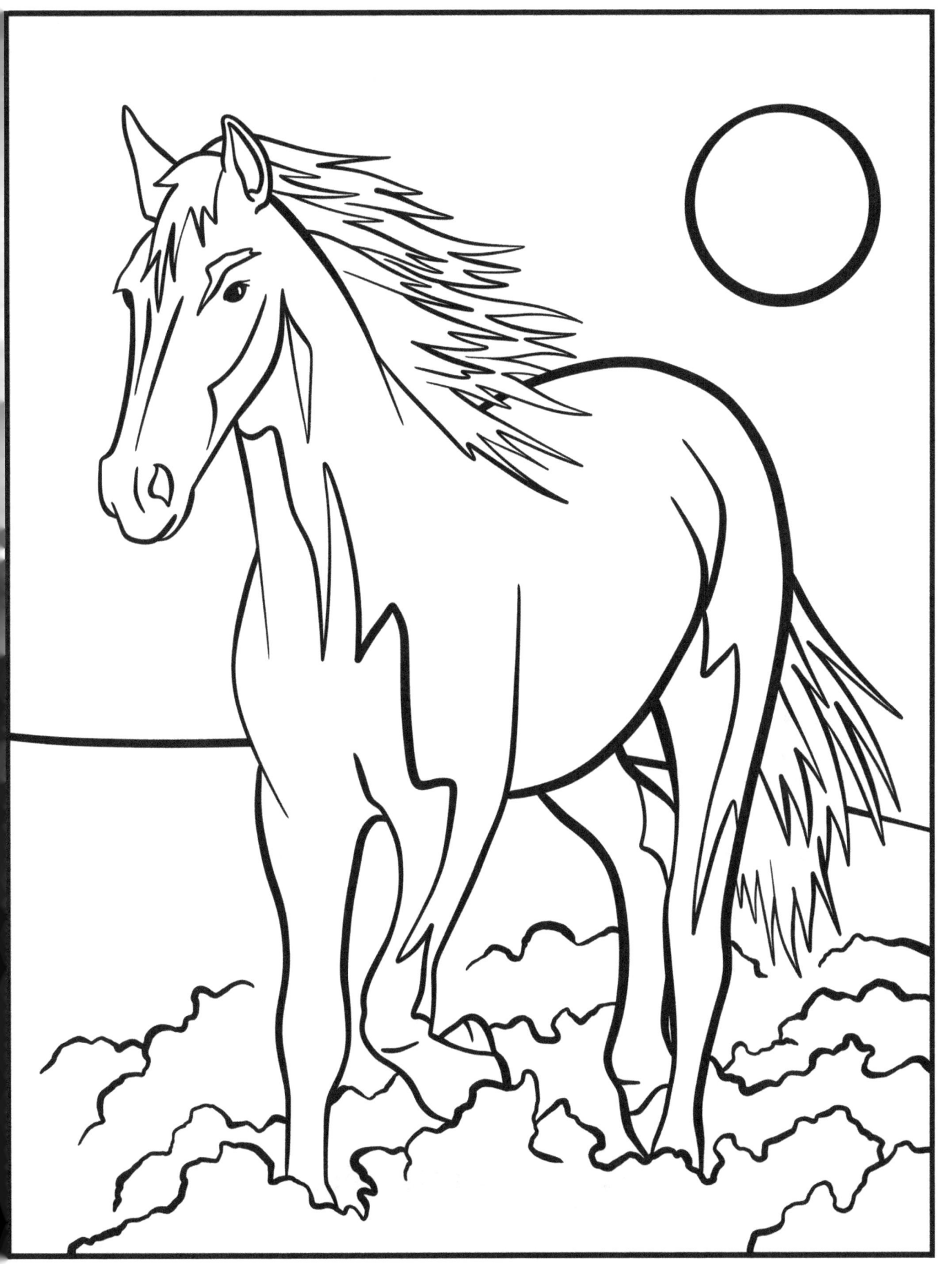

Kicking Up the Dirt

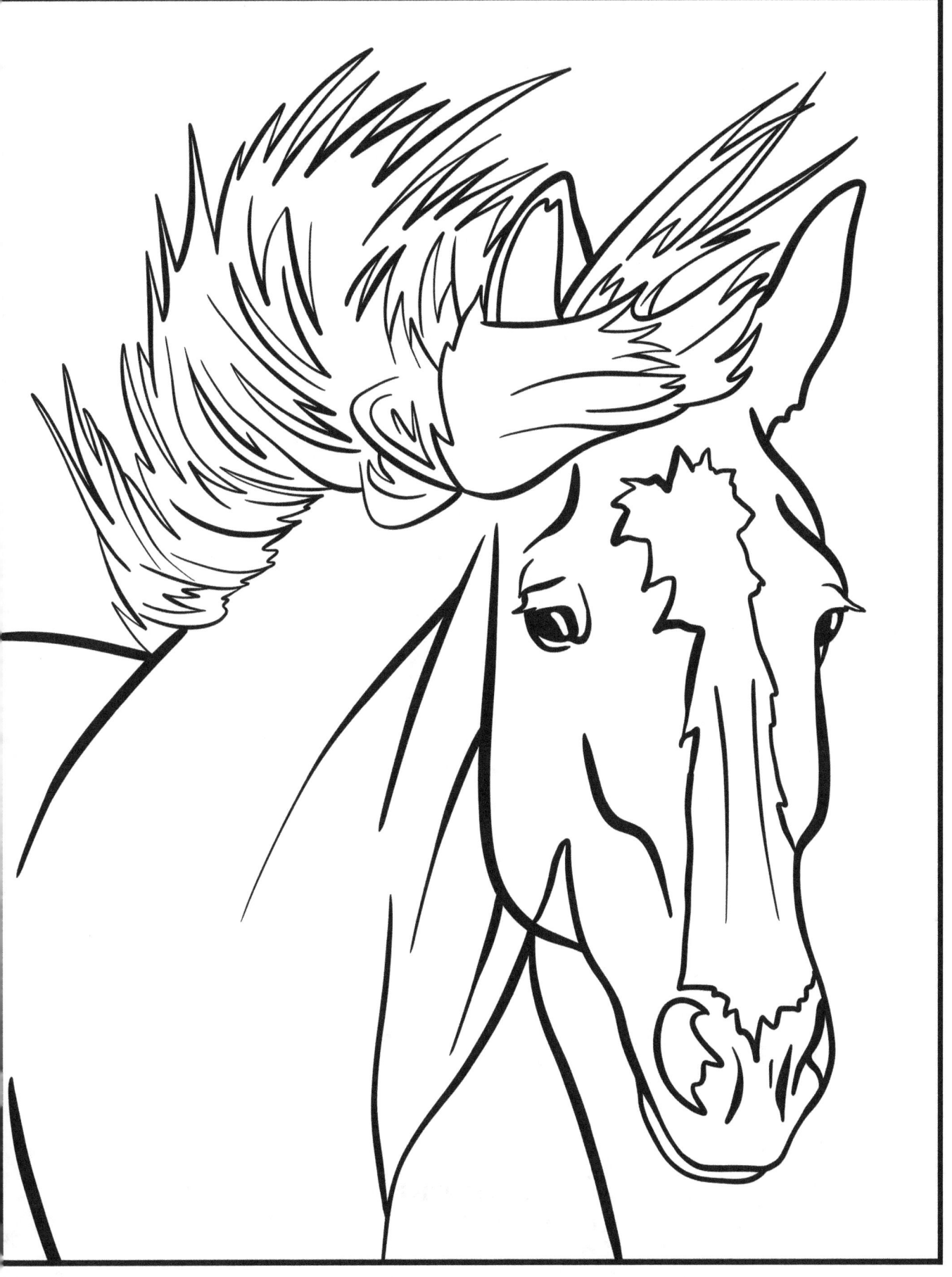

Running

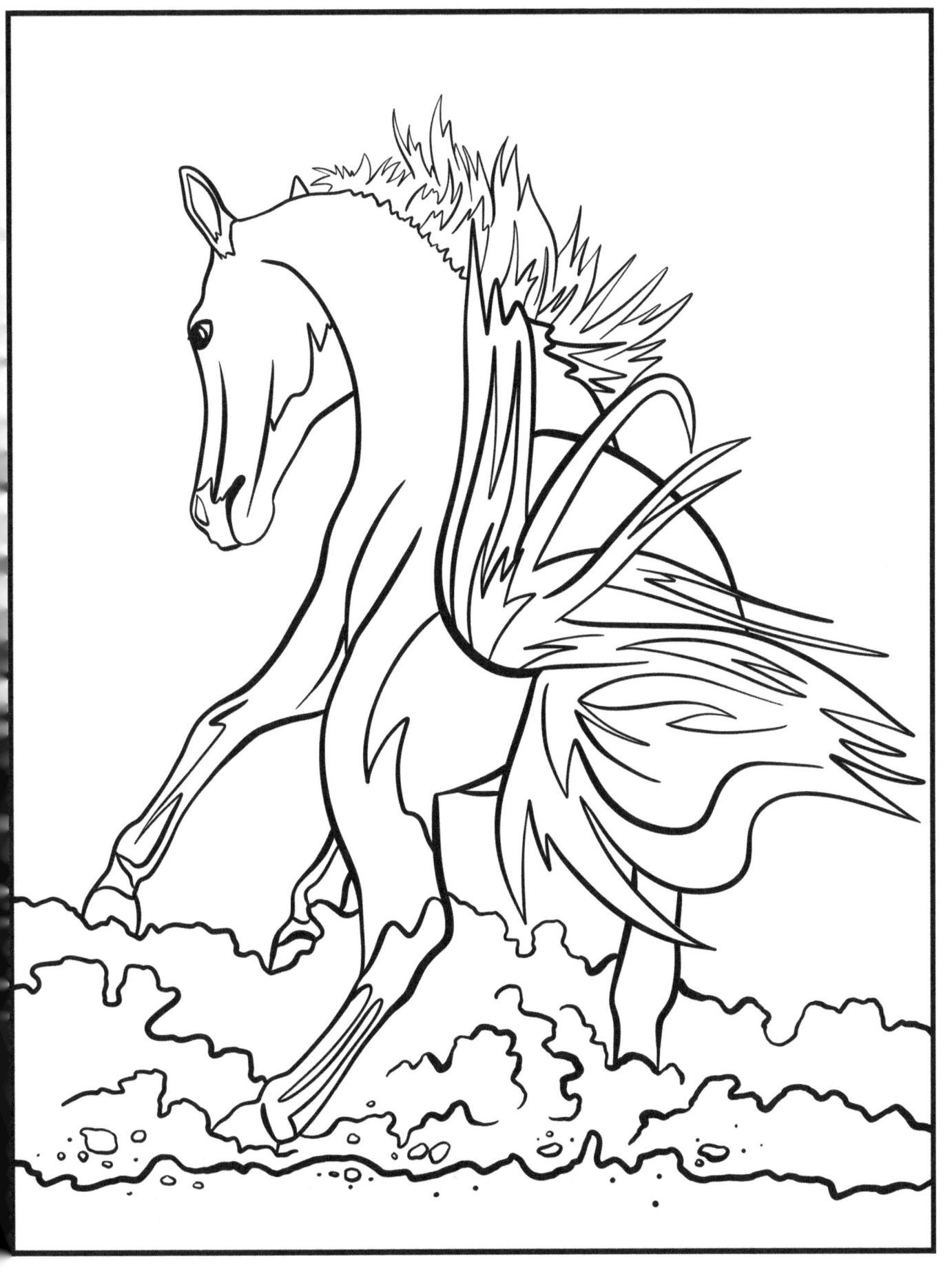

Wild Stallion

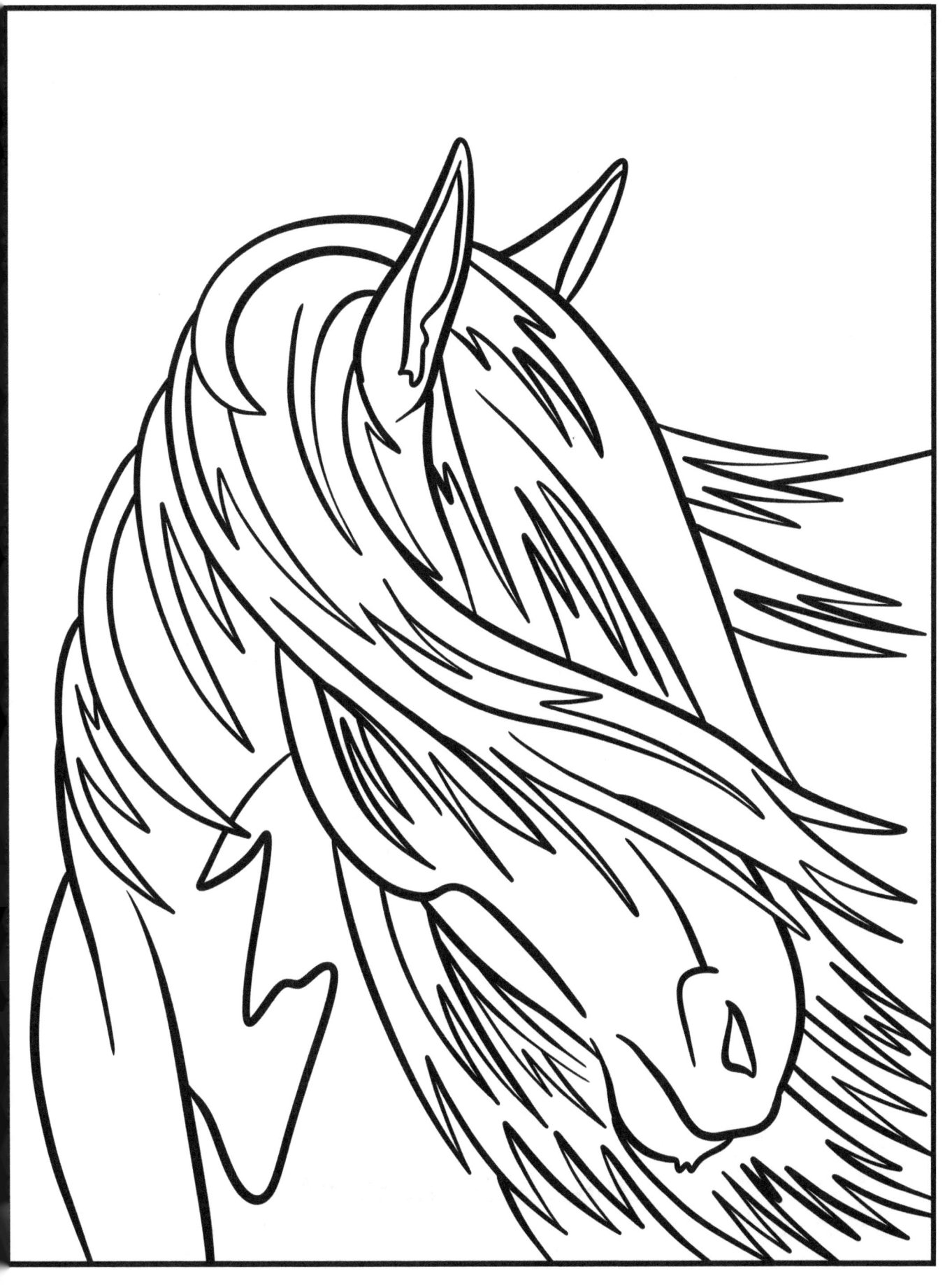

Blowing in the Wind

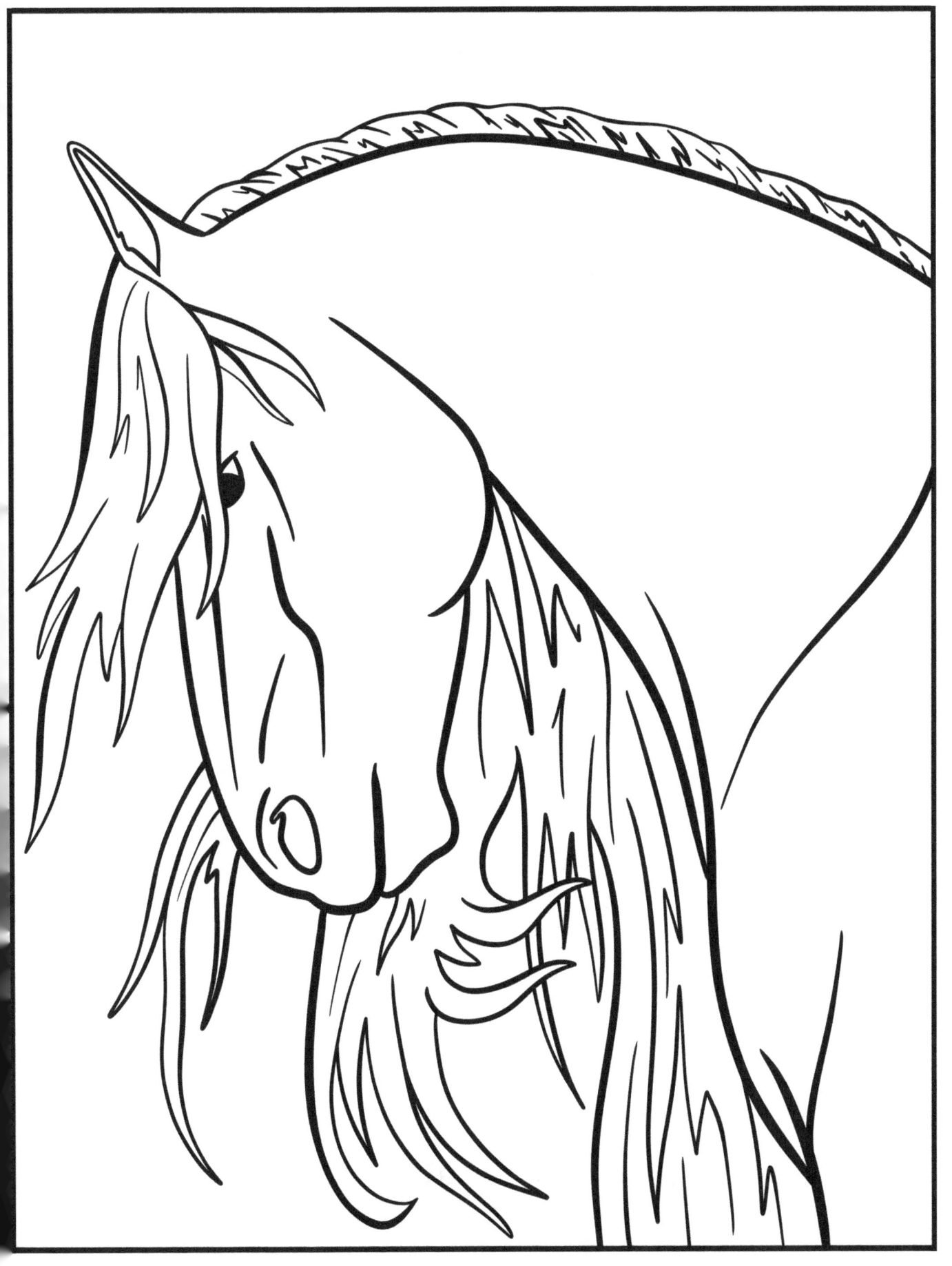

Strength

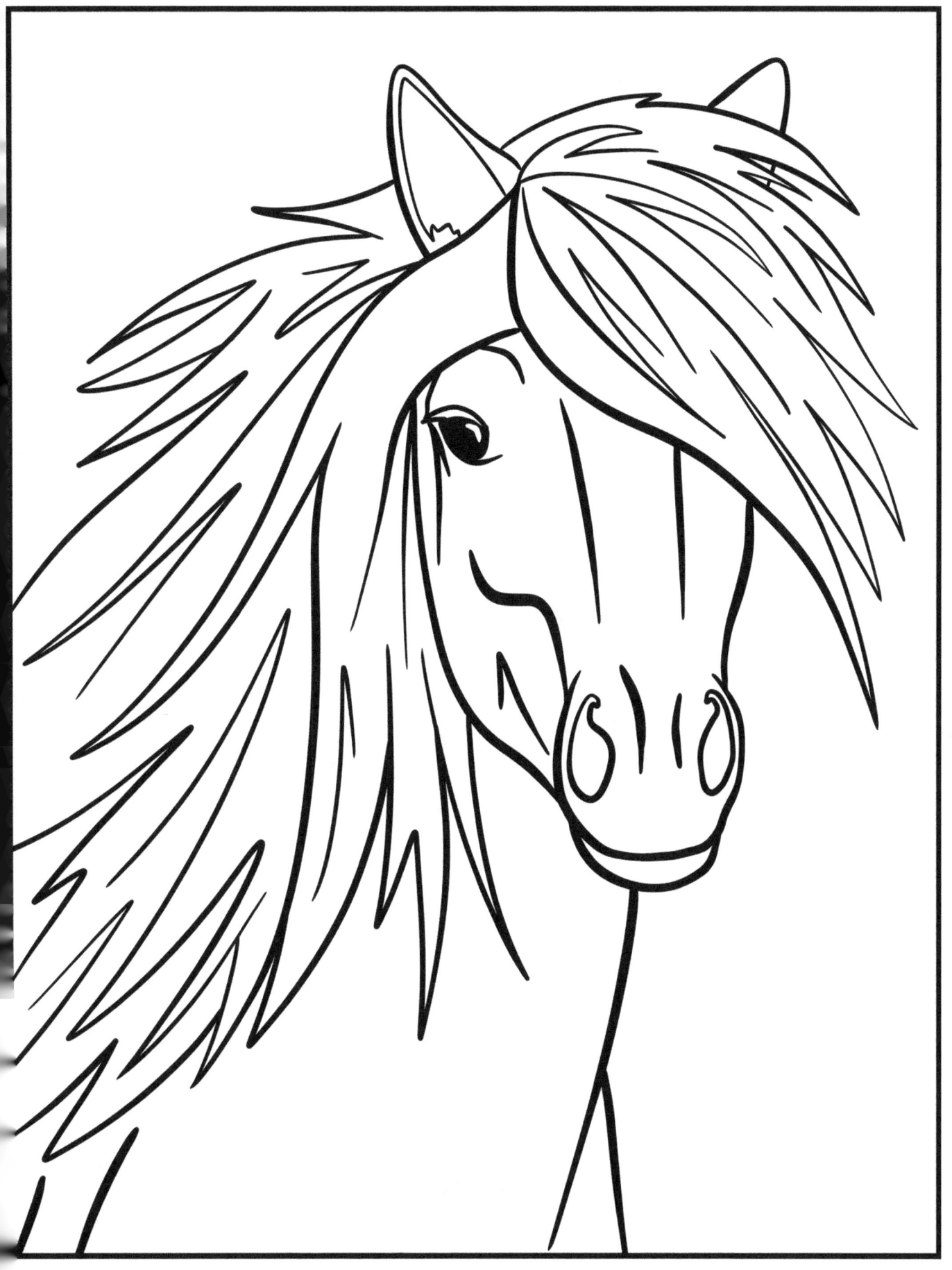

Youth

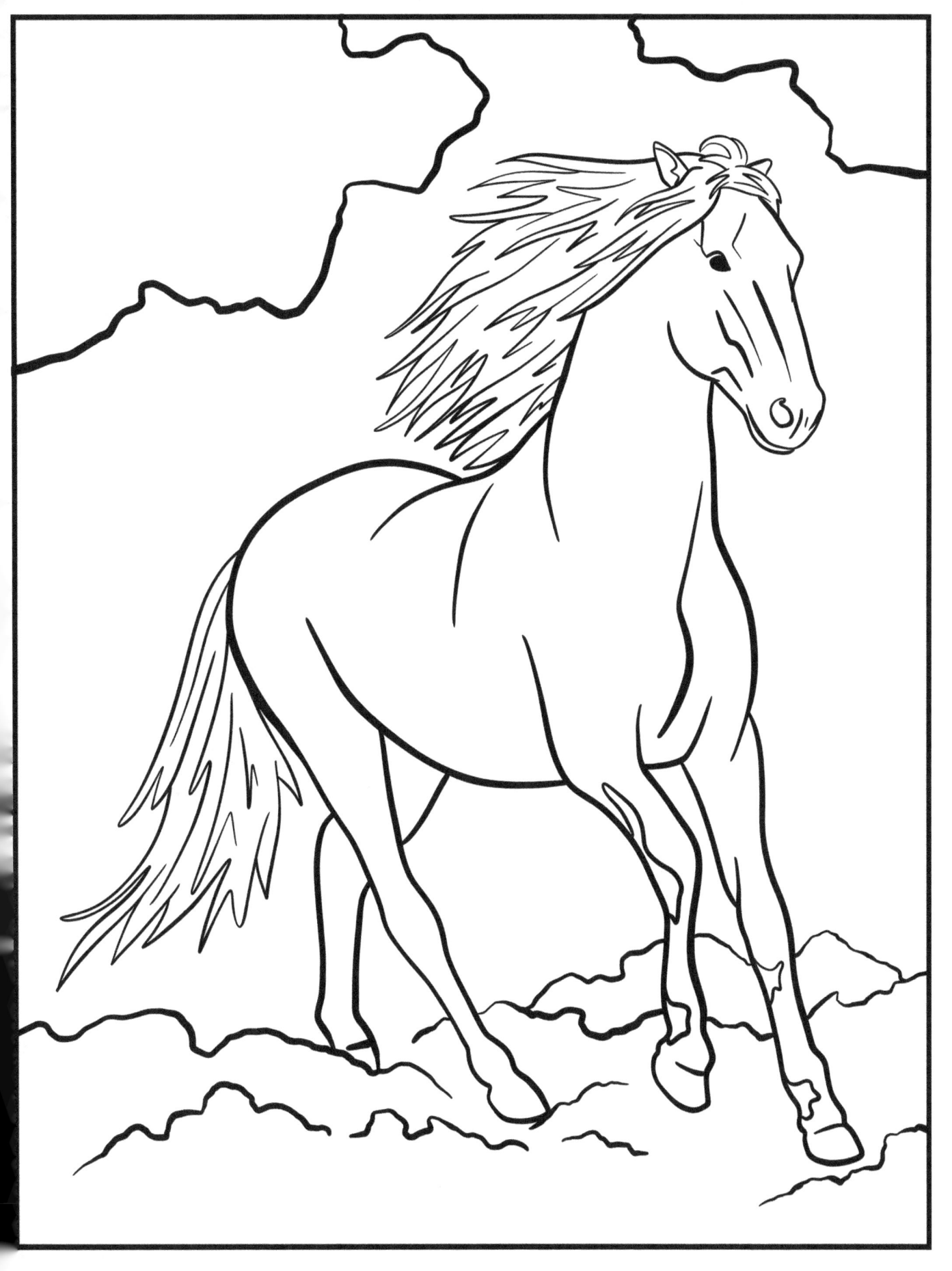

Freedom

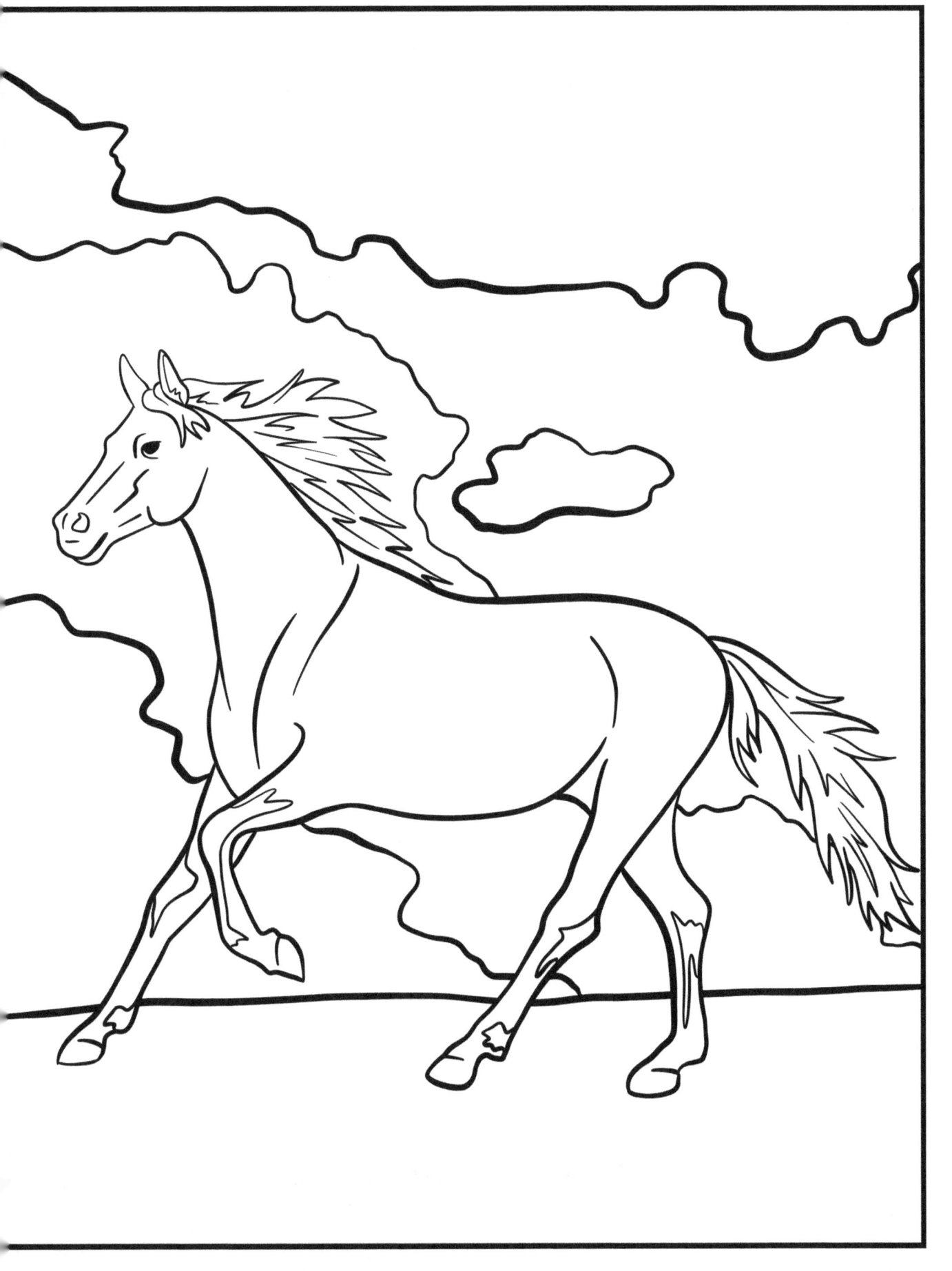

Running in the Grass

www.ingramcontent.com/pod-product-compliance
Lightning Source LLC
Chambersburg PA
CBHW080535220526
45465CB00006B/2709